Being Present
A Skill Worth Developing

Anila Trinlé

Being Present
A Skill Worth Developing

Anila Trinlé

Translated from the French by Jourdie Ross

The Knowledge Workshop

Special thanks from the translator to Cédric Georges, Louise Munoz,
Lama Puntso, and Michael Ross.

ISBN 979-10-93883-13-7

Table of Contents

Preface

This text is the result of encounters.

The meeting of Buddhism with other disciplines with an ongoing goal: discovering how Buddhism's values can shed light on our questions, how various disciplines, at times quite different from one another, can support each other in reaching greater clarity.

This is how we met researchers in the most varied of fields across the years: education, accompaniment, art, management, and even personal development and psychology. We questioned scholars and Buddhist masters. We encountered views that overlap and views that counter one another—in the end views that enrich one another.

This book also comes from encounters with people: Trinlé led and co-led dozens of training programs, seminars, and gatherings. Over the course of individual interviews, she heard multitudes of testimonials, life stories, and inquiries that force us to go further—to deepen our reflection, and which reveal the relevance or irrelevance of what is said.

Lastly, having been at her side throughout all this time of exploration, analysis, and quest for understanding, I can say that this text is the fruit of Trinlé's encounter with herself. By definition, when we seek, we do not know what we will find in the end. There are unknowns, hesitations, and also intuitions that must be validated through experience. This can only be accomplished by close personal commitment.

And then there is rigorousness. It is so easy to cherrypick aspects of reflection here and there, to mix up the data, to muddle the viewpoints, and to content oneself with an idea of innovation. It was important not to simply make a "soup" and to avoid squandering the Buddha's teaching on the pretext of rendering it concretely useful.

This first volume deals with being present. "Being present is a living process that reveals us to ourselves and, in so doing, allows us to connect with others in a new way." Being present is the basis of any action, which is why this series of handbooks begins with this particular theme. Here, we explore the theme through the process of accompanying others. At some point or another in our lives, we all find ourselves in the role of accompanying another.

This is not a book of recipes or a method for being more efficient day-to-day. This book gives us keys, openings, leads to follow so that our encounters with others (and, thus, with ourselves) may be fruitful. This text was not written to give answers, but rather to nurture our reflection.

Lama Puntso

Introduction

We can define being present as a way to be aware of what we experience. This presupposes a quality of awareness and an openness to what is happening, as much within ourselves as outside of ourselves. The ability to be present must be developed and refined. It is to be discovered and nurtured. Authentically being present thus involves training. It is not a fixed state. Various factors come into play, each demanding to be worked on. Being present is a process that reveals us to ourselves and thus allows us to connect with others in a new way. Developing this ability to be present refers less to questioning the situation than to questioning "me" in the situation.

In any relationship, notably when accompanying some-one dealing with suffering, being present in the right way comes from benevolent motivation, self awareness, and intelligent listening. It means allowing the other person to find their own autonomy in a supportive relationship.

To begin, let us look at the foundations of our approach. Clearly, the vision of the individual is a central point. In the Buddhist tradition, the vision of the individual and his environment differs from the Western perspective. A short presentation will give us an overview of this vision.

A Buddhist Approach to the Individual

The human being, rich in potential for wisdom and endowed with great qualities, is conscious and capable of experiencing things. This is in fact what defines it, but a way of functioning centered around itself limits the human being's way of knowing itself, others, and the world.

When we say "me," what does this actually refer to? We have a body, and through our senses—be it through sight, smell, sound, etc.—we have access to ourselves, to others, and to the environment that surrounds us. Sensations associated with concepts give us information and we subsequently identify and distinguish the perceived phenomena: from beings to objects to situations. Based on this, the emotions and various mental events that arise in the mind color our relationships to the objects of our perception.

For a single object of perception, the experience may be one of attraction or rejection, a feeling of superiority or inferiority, of comparison, of joyfulness, of openness, of worry, etc. according to the person. In the end, this results in an attitude made up of a mix of mental events that can be very sophisticated and that decide our reactions to the situations we encounter.

Thus, this "me" is an incessantly repeated identification with a body that is a support for sensory, mental, and emotional experiences. Seen through the filter of our mental habits, these experiences in turn make up our general experience of the world, others, and ourselves. This identification is called egocentric grasping—sometimes translated as ego, but this term leads to confusion because it does not refer to the same meaning as in the Western approach.

We identify ourselves with this way of knowing. In other words, we limit our knowledge by identifying ourselves with this process, while there is in fact more that can be known. "If we understand our situation, the conditions that we encounter, and their causes, then we will know that there is more to discover and that it concerns liberating ourselves from these conditions."[1]

Our way of knowing is thus conditioned by our perceptions and tendencies. This way of knowing is based on a misunderstanding that primarily concerns not seeing what truly is.

This way of functioning leads to dissonance. We are out of touch with reality. We take things that are interdependent and impermanent to be permanent, unique, and singular.

---

1   Lama Jigme Rinpoche, "The Thirty-Seven Practices of Bodhisattvas" (lecture series, St. Léon-sur-Vézère, France, 2006–2015)
Lama Jigme Rinpoche is an accomplished teacher in the Kagyu lineage, spiritual director of Dhagpo Kagyu Ling, and representative of the Gyalwa Karmapa in Europe.
Translator's Note: The audio files of this lecture series are available at the Dhagpo Kagyu Library in St. Léon-sur-Vezère, France. Further reading can also be found in his book based on this same series of lectures: Lama Jigme Rinpoche, The Handbook of Ordinary Heroes: The Bodhisattvas' Way (La Remuée: Rabsel Éditions, 2016).

Interdependence

What does this mean? We take things that are composite and that depends on causes and circumstances to be singular and autonomous. In fact, nothing that exists is independent or autonomous.

For example, let us take a few moments to look at what causes and circumstances had to come together in order for each of us today to be a human being capable of taking care of ourself in life. First, we obviously had a father and mother who conceived us and took care of us to help us survive, and also took care of our education, teaching us life lessons, etc. Then, we had to gain our own experience in professional, relational, and family settings. In order to be, today, what we consider autonomous, we relied on numerous people, numerous supports, and myriad circumstances.

Furthermore, for us to have a father and mother capable of raising us, they likewise had to have numerous causes and circumstances, parents, etc... We can reach back infinitely without ever finding a single thing that has existed without depending on something else.

Another aspect of interdependence is that numerous causes and conditions must come together for something to occur at a precise moment. Consider an example: for a play to take place, there must be a playwright, actors, a theater, technicians, a ticket booth, an audience, publicity, etc. If one of these elements is absent, the play does not take place! Without a stage, without a set, without a curtain to go up, without lights or sound: no play. Without actors: no play. Without a ticket booth: no play, etc. If all of these elements do not come together at the same time in a given place, there is no play.

So it is for all phenomena. Nothing takes place without being dependent on various other parameters. Parameters that are themselves variable, subject to change, and that resist any form of control. In this way, everything is composite and impermanent. Nothing is fixed or definitive. This is what we call interdependence and what calls into question our vision of ourselves and the world.

Impermanence

Although we are aware of our mortality, we experience ourselves as being permanent in the moment. We have the feeling of being lasting; "me" seems to exist forcefully as a permanent entity.

However, we are well aware that everything that has a beginning ends one day; everything that is born dies. We know this intellectually, but our experience does not take into account this unavoidable fact of our reality.

As such, we seek out and construct our happiness by acquiring what we like—everything that pleases us, interests us, and reassures us—without considering its impermanence. If we look closely, we construct our happiness on a foundation of sand thinking that we are building it on solid, stable ground.

We only have access to the visible effects of impermanence; for example, our child growing up, a project failing, an adult aging, our neighborhood being renovated. But we do not have access to the reality of impermanence through our senses. For something to change, it must change from moment to moment. A child does not grow up all at once. He grows up because his body transforms from moment to moment as he grows.

A building is not new for a certain period of time and then suddenly becomes dilapidated and collapses. For a building to become a dilapidated ruin, the breakdown must occur from moment to moment, little by little, over time.

If we consider that time is nothing more than a succession of moments, we will observe that the present moment generates the following one. A change—a transformation—can therefore only occur from moment to moment. For example, a flower that blooms, an egg that hatches, a sky that becomes overcast; we can observe progressive transformations in these things. But how do we observe a new house progressively transforming into a ruin? It is impossible, but it is not because we cannot perceive it with our senses that it does not take place.

In fact, we are trapped by our own way of functioning, which leads us to solidify what we feel and perceive and to make it static. We take things that are naturally uncertain and impermanent to be stable and definitive.

It is only through reflection that we can have access to the reality of impermanence. This means reflecting, not on the visible effects of impermanence, but on this "mechanism" of successive moments that generates changes.

It would be mistaken to only see the unpleasant aspects of impermanence. It is likewise because things change from moment to moment that we can acquire new skills, that we can establish ourselves in various domains, and that we can develop our potential. It is through a slow effort of transformation that we can work toward greater clarity and kindness.

But we like certain effects of impermanence, and we reject others. We accept birth but not death, the end of an illness but not the diagnosis, the beginning of a relationship but not a separation, etc. This is because of the attachment to what is convenient to us and the rejection of what bothers us.

It is due to awareness of impermanence that we can welcome what arises within us little by little —be it disturbing emotions, ideas, fears, or hopes: because we know that its nature is unstable and volatile. It is due to this knowledge that we can transform a moment of being closed off to one of openness, a moment of rejection into one of welcoming, and a moment of anger into one of calm.

We have the opportunity here to reflect on this reality. We sometimes have the feeling that reflecting on impermanence is rather morbid, that it is preferable not to think about how we will one day be separated from those we love. But knowledge of this aspect of reality is far from being solely a source of suffering. When we know that we only have access to something for a certain amount of time, we enjoy what is there without becoming attached to it in the same way.

For example, when it snows, particularly in a region where snow is rare, all the children (and even the adults) run gleefully outside to have snowball fights or build snowmen because they know that it will not last. Maybe when the snow has melted there is some regret that it did not last longer, but there is no real distress.

The example of snow may seem lighthearted, without any real substance, but it allows us to see that on many occasions we do know how to interact with the world while taking change into account. And furthermore, it is because we are aware of their impermanence that we experience certain situations in an intense, meaningful way.

It is very likely that when we have assimilated the nature of this reality that we are a part of—in other words that we are subject to change—we will take it to heart to make every moment of our life a moment of opening that leads us to our chosen goal. And we will do so without rushing, but with awareness of the preciousness of the present moment.

Furthermore, most of our suffering is connected to

the fact that we become attached to people, objects, and situations without considering their impermanence. Reflecting on impermanence allows us to establish relationships with more openness, that are more generous, and particularly more connected to our reality.

Happiness and Pleasure;
Suffering and Dissatisfaction

In our desire to be happy, we confuse pleasure with happiness, on the one hand, and dissatisfaction with suffering, on the other. Our search to acquire and retain the things that suit us is likewise somewhat frenetic and leads us to accumulate many actions that cause suffering sooner or later. In addition, we experience things that upset us or leave us dissatisfied as a form of suffering.

The search for immediate or near-immediate pleasure and the rejection of things that disturb us conditions our vision of happiness. However, in order to educate a child, for example, we must sometimes upset the child by forbidding him from doing things that will theoretically bring him pleasure but that are dangerous. What is, in this case, an immediate source of dissatisfaction in fact brings about happiness in the longterm. In the same way, giving sugar to a diabetic generates immediate pleasure but has harmful consequences sooner or later.

We tend to consider the immediate effects of our actions without always considering their longterm effects on our minds or on others. The more clarity we have regarding the goal we wish to achieve, the better equipped we will be to put up with temporary dissatisfaction.

Consider the example of a skier: becoming a champion requires hours and hours of training, of physical suffering and psychological challenges. But because he wishes to attain his goal—to become a champion—all of these difficulties and dissatisfaction are not suffering but training!

Through this, we get a glimpse of how motivation underlies and supports all our actions, be they actions of body, speech, or mind. Thus the importance of clarifying our motivation; this is an important key concept of the reflection on being present.

We have seen that the being we are is endowed with a potential for discernment and kindness that is rich with vast qualities. At the same time, however, its way of experiencing the world—conditioned by self-centered functioning—limits and creates obstacles to the perception of reality. This produces a vision of reality that does not take essential parameters such as interdependence and impermanence into account and, moreover, one that generates a troubled relationship to pleasure and dissatisfaction. These are the reflections we need to carry out—veritable resources for heading toward greater clarity.

Accompanying Others

We often associate accompanying others with difficult periods in life. And yet, different individuals have accompanied us all throughout our lives. Perhaps someone is currently accompanying us, and someone certainly will later in life. Whether it is over the course of our education, during temporary difficulties or illness, or likewise through joyful discoveries, the people who accompanied us have allowed us to become who we are today.

In the same way, in our daily lives, in our professional, personal, and circumstantial relationships, we can take an approach of accompanying those around us.

When we are with someone, we apply our attention and awareness in a specific way according to the situation, our position, and the issues at hand.

In the context of accompanying a person who is suffering, we will be attentive to our listening; in a professional setting, we will perhaps focus our attention on what is at stake; in a personal situation, we will be more vigilant about maintaining a quality relationship while taking our shared history into account.

Accompanying Someone Suffering from Illness and/or at the End of Life

The word "accompany" comes from the ancient word "*compain*," which means to share bread. If we place this word back in its medieval context where the Christian faith was very present, we see that people associated the symbolism of bread with life. We are talking about the bread of life. Therefore, we can directly understand "accompanying" to mean "sharing a moment of life."

Accompanying also means walking with someone, and this implies following another's rhythm, matching our pace to his or hers. In other words, accepting another's choices and respecting his or her values and priorities. The notion of respecting another's rhythm is essential but not always easy to apply. Though we may have good intentions, there is great risk of offering our own answers to a situation to which we are merely a witness. We often have difficulty facing our inability to concretely ease others' suffering.

We often feel powerless, and this leads us to reply out of discomfort, without taking into account the actual needs of the person we are accompanying.

Accompanying is also knowing how to listen, how to hear beyond the words themselves in order to be more open to another person. Listening requires us to be available—as much internally as externally—and flexible. Listening also demands that we be more attentive to the experience of the individual than to the objectivity of the facts. We can remind ourselves that in these circumstances, each of us only has access to his or her own representation of the situation. It is not because another's vision is quite different than our own that it is not important for him or her. We can also reflect on the fact that both our vision and the other person's are equally subjective and limited! But our vision is all that is available to us, and we interact with others based on this vision. The idea is to try to perceive the situation from the point of view of the person we are accompanying, without offering a solution, but simply allowing him or her to find his or her own answers through kind and attentive listening.

But accompanying someone is not only a skill we must have; it is first and foremost a way of being, and we must cultivate this way of being. When we talk about being present with someone who is suffering, this in fact means being aware of what we experience in the moment we are present itself. It also means developing awareness of what the accompanied person is experiencing, all while being present to their environment—as much physical as relational.

Being aware of what we experience implies reflection on our motivation and reliance on our resources—developing those that are weak and acquiring those that we lack. It also means accepting facing our fears, our disturbing emotions, our expectations, and our disappointment to move toward greater clarity.

The Various Types of Support Relationships

When we are in the presence of a sick person or someone at the end of life, it is important to be aware of our position because, according to our role or position, the context and the limits may differ. We chose to distinguish six main types of roles, each one with its own specificity.

Each type of relationship—be it a temporary support relationship, one that is therapeutic, psychotherapeutic, of volunteer accompaniment, spiritual, or personal—requires certain skills and implies a specific commitment.

A temporary support relationship focuses on a problem that needs to be resolved. It is an immediate form of aid that requires common sense, care for the person involved, generosity, and pragmatism. Examples of this include taking care of the neighbor's cat while he is in the hospital or helping someone file administrative papers, etc.

The therapeutic relationship centers around an ill person and/or the illness of the person. This concerns health professionals in the widest sense of the term. It relates to treatment—offering appropriate further care after diagnosis and prescription, as well as to care taking—acting with particular attention and awareness to give one's treatment a human aspect of generosity and kindness. Naturally, this relationship requires training and the corresponding skill set according to the various fields of care.

The psychotherapeutic relationship centers around the relationship itself with the goal being a process of repair and reconstruction. It begins based on the explicit request of the client. The process differs according to different types of psychotherapy—and there are many, but this always requires serious training and, most of the time, supervision.

The relationship of accompanying someone as a volunteer centers around the person. Based on listening and being present, it offers a space to work through difficulties—to find his or her own answers or adjustments—for the person being accompanied. The volunteer must receive training within an organization that provides him or her with follow-up in the form of discussion groups led by competent individuals.

The spiritual relationship centers around transcendence

in the widest sense of the term. It is simultaneously based on intelligence and heart, confidence and discernment. It allows us to go beyond appearances and, in the case of the Buddhist path, beyond duality. In every case, it requires guidance that supports the process of transformation. The guide must have personal experience of the path proposed by his or her own spiritual tradition.

The personal relationship centers around experience, shared history, what is at stake and the emotional rapport built of love and attachment, but also doubts, sometimes wounds, and often irritations... In fact our relationships with our loved ones are often ambivalent and create joy, sadness, and affection, but also anger, guilt, etc... In fact, we feel a cocktail of emotions that are often pleasant but also at times explosive toward those close to us! The particularity of this relationship is that it can take on different aspects— whether on the concrete, material level or in terms of care— but it cannot be compared to a volunteer relationship nor a psychotherapeutic one because of the limits imposed by attachment, the issues at hand, the past, etc. Furthermore, in this context, the suffering of the person accompanied has a deep impact on the person accompanying. This zeroes in on our own suffering, which is not the case in other types of relationships.

As we just saw, each type of relationship is different. Each relationship has its place and its role for someone who is suffering. The most important point is to be clear on our own position. This is what allows us to experience limits in terms of magnitude and not in terms of limitation. In addition, being honest about this is necessary in relation to the other person.

Accompanying Someone Who is Grieving

The simplest definition of grieving is this: the process of adapting to a new situation.

This process takes place in every situation of loss or separation, be it the death of a loved one, the end of a relationship, the loss of an object we care about, or unemployment, but also the end of a project, the failure of a dream, etc.

Accompanying a person who is grieving requires a good knowledge of the process of grief, and we won't go into detail here. However, one thing to keep in mind is that a description of grief in several stages is a tool rather than an undeniable process. Though the process of grief is universal, we experience it in a unique and singular way each time based on a great number of parameters connected to the circumstances of loss, the loss itself, and the personality of the grieving person.

No matter what, accompanying a person who is grieving requires very sharp attention and awareness as the suffering of loss brings with it a vulnerability that is important to take into account. The path of grieving may be long, is often difficult, always painful and requires discretion, sensitivity, and kindness on the part of the person accompanying.

As we have seen, accompanying someone requires skill—a capacity to act based partly on greater clarity of our role in the situation—and of course also a way of being.

The first step for developing the ability to be present and aware of what is happening is to clarify our motivation.

Motivation

Why?

The foundation for being present is motivation. Our motivation orients our presence, gives it strength, and allows us to remain present longterm. Motivation is at the heart of any approach; it conditions our way of being in the world. Why we do things determines how we do things. Our motivation is always made up of our life history and the concepts and beliefs that accompany them. Our emotions and mental habits color our motivation; our need for recognition and our expectations also influence it. Our kindness, our patience, and our interest in others likewise contribute to it. All of our everyday motivations— at times emotional, at times generous, sometimes very clear, sometimes rather confused—make up our general motivation.

Our various motivations are a prime opportunity to come face to face with ourselves.

Nothing that we do, that we think, or that we conceptualize is separate from our motivation. When we talk about motivation, we are talking about this profound movement within us that is an expression of our vision of the world, which makes us act, think, reflect, and speak.

In order to begin this reflection, we must first clarify our vision of ourselves, the world, and our relationship to others. For each of us, the things that make up our motivation differ. This is important to consider: various expectations contribute to our motivation. Some of them are rather tricky, such as a natural but sometimes overwrought need for recognition, which is further made up of various objectives to accomplish and aspirations to satisfy, etc. In fact, our motivation is the expression of our vision and our conceptions.

Our conception of a situation plays into everything we do. It determines what we think we should be in the situation and how the other should react in the relationship. How much awareness do we have of this conception and are we conscious of the fact that it is only our version of the situation?

What is my vision of myself? How do I conceptualize

the world? What do I expect of my relationships? Who do I want to be in the world? Why have I committed to reflecting on being present for others and myself?

Such questions allow us to clarify our motivation. However, it is important to keep in mind that certain fundamental aspects of our motivation are barely accessible to us in the beginning. They come from our personal history, our tendencies, our beliefs, and our way of conceptualizing, which are not always very clear.

Furthermore, it is easy to see that our motivation is unstable, impermanent. Some days we are ready to take on all kinds of obstacles to accomplish some thing or another and other times we have trouble just getting out of bed... What motivates us one day does not even interest us some time later. Why? Maybe because certain aspects of our motivation have not been nurtured according to our expectations, so we no longer take an interest in a particular activity.

Let's look at an example:

Jack starts his new job with energy and enthusiasm. He has been dreaming about participating in the development of a project to support schools in an underprivileged neighborhood. He has reflected a lot on the different kinds of funding possible and how to encourage parents and kids to take part in the program. However, some time later, we find Jack discouraged and ready to quit his job. Too many disappointments and too much disillusionment have challenged his project.

One way to understand this discouragement is to look at Jack's motivation. Of course, his initial enthusiasm included generosity and the joy of being able to apply his skills and share his experience. But Jack also had a natural expectation of recognition for his work. In addition, he hoped that his work would win him back his family's respect after their reproach of his recent unemployment. Furthermore, he had a very specific idea of how relationships with the youths should occur. This was all subconscious, even tinged with the idea that things should happen "like this." However, Jack's bosses more or less ignored his efforts, his loved ones disparaged his work, and his relationships with the youths were relatively tense and, from his point of view, fruitless.

By analyzing this situation, we can see how much our motivation is central to our way of experiencing events in our lives.

Furthermore, our motivation is not stable and can lead us away from our initial goal without our really noticing.

Simon is a history professor who is passionate about the Middle Ages. He is also a generous man who especially appreciates sharing his knowledge. At the start of term, he is content, speaks enthusiastically, and sees the interest that his students have in his classes. Little by little, he becomes more and more concerned with entertaining his listeners.

He begins to listen to himself speak and seek approval of his presentation rather than an interest in the content he transmits. Without realizing it, his attention shifts more and more toward his need for recognition, despite the fact that generosity and a wish to share his knowledge were initially his priority. He finishes the term disappointed and questions his ability to teach as well as the abilities of his students to learn his subject

Looking at this example, we can see how easy it is to react by blaming others or feeling guilty. Only if we make an effort to determine what generates such disappointments do we have the ability to do something about them. We should rejoice in being disappointed because although it is uncomfortable, it allows us to see our subconscious expectations.

In his book *Cutting Through Spiritual Materialism*, Chogyam Trungpa says, "Disappointment is a good sign of basic intelligence. It cannot be compared to anything else: it is so sharp, precise, obvious, and direct. If we can open, then we suddenly begin to see that our expectations are irrelevant compared with the reality of the situations we are facing. This automatically brings a feeling of disappointment."[2]

Disappointment is indeed an excellent entry point for

---

2   Chogyam Trungpa Rinpoche, *Cutting Through Spiritual Materialism* (Boston: Shambala Publications, Inc., 1973), 25.
Chogyam Trungpa Rinpoche was a Tibetan Buddhist master.

discovering the different parameters that make up our motivation, verifying their relevance, and thus clarifying what drives us. What goal do we wish to attain and what means are we willing to use to achieve it? Because this is indeed the question: "What do I want in the end?"

What is my conception of happiness? And is this vision coherent with the reality of our world?

We could summarize these questions as "why" and "for what" we accomplish certain activities and not others. What is the basis of our motivation and what direction do we wish to take? Where are we coming from and where are we going?

These things are not always very clear to us because we often do things out of habit, automatically. We have difficulty seeing how our way of interacting with a given situation develops because it seems obvious to us that "this" is how one should approach it. We are subject to our conceptions, our beliefs, and our biases without considering them consciously. This is natural because such consideration is not immediately available to us. This is why disappointment is an ally: because it reveals our unseen expectations to us.

What For?

Motivation likewise brings up the question of a more

fundamental "what for?" What are we ultimately seeking; what is our aim in the longterm? We may experience and do things with the goal of being happy or at least being happier. We may have a wider perspective with a spiritual aim: based on our own liberation or based on the wish to bring benefit for all beings, for example.

For some people, this "what for" remains vague. For others, it gives meaning to their lives. Either way, these two levels of motivation will permeate each other. To be able to be truly present, clarifying our motivation again and again is the primary condition.

If we are aware of the complexities of relationships and interested in being useful to beings and the world, we can make the wish to be a "good human" who is generous and caring—a "good person" who acts based on humanity imbued with altruistic values.

Having encountered the limits of our conceptions and emotions, we can cultivate the wish to break out of a way of functioning that generates dissatisfaction and suffering. We can instead make the wish to be free.

Having seen that all beings wish to be happy and being conscious of their suffering, we can make the profound wish that we and all beings may be liberated from dissatisfaction and suffering and that we may experience happiness and its causes. In the Buddhist teaching, we call this bodhicitta or enlightened mind.

Whatever our goal may be, reminding ourselves of our objective allows us to accept imperfect situations and to find the courage needed to surpass difficulties. We are capable of doing so because it has meaning for us. In this way, all setbacks become part of a process of development and clarification. We experience them less like obstacles and more like steps in our training.

We become like an athlete who pushes himself to run faster and longer to the point that he reaches exhaustion and physical pain, but who no longer associates it with suffering but simply training to reach his goal: to win the race!

Therefore, clarifying our motivation means, on one hand, discovering our way of functioning and, on the other, clearly defining the goal we wish to attain.

Attention and Awareness

Being present requires several of the mind's capacities: attention, awareness, and taking care.

Attention, or the ability to remember something, means being able to remain conscious of what we want and what we do not want. "There are choices upon choices taking place constantly. Attending to those choices and their reference points is known as recollection, *smriti* in Sanskrit. This is not exactly bringing the past to the present, but still in order to be in the present, you need memory[.]"[3]

Habits are part of what make us up, and many choices occur without our being conscious of them—automatically.

---

3 Chogyam Trungpa Rinpoche, *The Path is the Goal: A Basic Handbook of Buddhist Meditation* (Boston: Shambhala South Asia Editions, 2000), 73.

If we are not clear on our motivation and we do not manage to keep it in mind, there is a major possibility that our actions will not be appropriate and we will reap unwanted results.

Awareness is defined in terms of "surveying." Traditional Buddhist texts speak about, "the repeated examination in all circumstances [...] of our physical, verbal, and mental behavior, and the conscious implementation of the principle of adopting what is to be done and rejecting what is not to be done."[4] This idea of surveying can give an impression of constraints or a lack of spontaneity. Basing our actions on what is correct (by remembering) and staying with our choices up through their realization (through awareness) is a self-aware and open state of mind that we must develop. Together with the ability to remember, awareness gives us greater freedom and allows us to move in a desired direction.

---

4 Kunzang Pelden, *The Nectar of Manjushri's Speech: A Detailed Commentary on Shantideva's Way of the Bodhisattva* (Boston and London: Shambhala, 2007), 164.

Taking Care

And now, "taking care." One way to express this is "non-neglect." In this context, taking care means bringing together the conditions to create real benefit for oneself and others. Without attention and awareness, we cannot develop the thoughtful care that allows us to liberate ourselves from obstacles and conditioning to be more open to others.

Taking care is a matter of application, of putting it into practice. Our observation of what arises within us allows us to verify its relevance. Little by little, taking care helps us make our daily life a path of clarity—of connection with ourselves and kindness toward others.

What is Taking Care?

Laying the foundation for being present means simultaneously cultivating an awareness of oneself, an awareness of the other person's experience, and an awareness of the surrounding environment. To begin, we will consider what is happening for us in this approach. To be able to apply the means necessary to be present for others, we must look at our own way of functioning before considering what we might offer others.

Taking care is a state of mind we can bring to every situation, be it professional, interpersonal, in a process of accompaniment, or simply in daily life. "Taking care of ourselves means relying on our own intelligence to be present and aware, thus avoiding limitless suffering. [...] When the Buddha speaks of taking care of oneself, he points to being aware of oneself among others."[5]

"Taking care" may have different connotations according to the context and vision we apply to it.

It is interesting to consider this notion in the case of a nurse, wherein taking care adds an aspect of particular awareness and attention to the verb "care." It connects the care given—which comes from knowledge—to a generous state of mind, which relates to a way of being.

---

5   Lama Jigme Rinpoche; see Footnote 1 for full citation and further reading.

For a sick person, being taken care of means feeling that he or she counts for the person caring for him or her. It means feeling as though one exists as an individual within the often worrying context of the medical system. And, for those doing the caring, it is a way to express their kindness based on their professional skills and with respect for the patient.

In the context of daily life, taking care of something means being attentive to keeping it in good condition. Consider an example: taking care of a garden. This concerns both maintaining the existing plants, sowing or planting new species, weeding, watering, fertilizing, etc. Taking care of a garden means using one's energy and knowledge to achieve an intended result while taking into account the environmental conditions and needs of each plant. It means applying careful attention and awareness to allow different plants to flourish in the proper conditions for their growth.

In the Buddhist context, "taking care" refers to precise ideas and relies on inherent human qualities. We can talk about it in terms of non-neglect and careful attention. What does this mean?

As we have seen, clarifying our motivation and the meaning we wish to bring to our spiritual path is crucial. Relying on attention and awareness, we are conscientious about respecting our ethic, that of not ignoring the little (or big) negativities of daily life.

The key notion of Buddhist ethics can be summarized in three words: not causing harm. But being attentive to not causing harm requires developing awareness of what causes harm—as much in terms of visible, immediate effects on ourselves and others as in terms of consequences for our own minds.

For example, the more we react based on impatience or anger in the face of opposition, the more this reaction arises in any circumstance; the more it will be spontaneous and become a habit and a tendency we are subject to without much awareness. However, if we wish to respect our chosen ethic—that is "not causing harm"—we can see that if we do this we are straying from the path. Not only is it unpleasant for those around us, but this habit distances us from our goal.

The idea of negative or positive action is in no way moral. It concerns whether or not what we are doing, saying, or thinking brings us closer to or takes further away from our goal: breaking free from a way of functioning that generates suffering. This requires knowledge of the goal and the means to be successful as well as attentive awareness.

Taking care in the context of the Buddhist path is in fact taking care of our minds—being conscious of our actions and making an effort to cultivate memory and awareness. This means remembering what to avoid and what method or teaching to apply, as well as being vigilant in doing so.

To allow us to be present to the reality of the experiences we encounter, the Buddha's teaching proposes that we develop greater awareness of our own way of functioning. Attention and awareness are definite allies for cultivating greater clarity about our motivation, concepts, and emotions.

The careful attention that we bring to what arises within us allows us to verify its relevance according to our own discernment. Little by little, this training allows us to make our daily life a path toward clarity, toward greater connection with ourselves, and toward kindness for others. In fact, becoming aware of what arises within us is a way to take care of ourselves.

In this way, it becomes clear that taking care is above all an attitude of attentiveness and kindness that supports and accompanies professional work, personal relationships, or an educational approach. This way of looking at daily life allows us to bring diverse situations to the spiritual path.

However, while the modern idea of "taking care of yourself" often implies being gentle with ourselves, pampering ourselves, and respecting and enforcing our limits, this is not the case here. "Taking care" in the Buddhist tradition means respecting our own ethics, cultivating an appropriate state of mind, and being careful not to fall victim to our own tendency to react to situations emotionally and in a self-centered way.

So that shakes up the norm! To understand this vision, it is important to understand that the Buddha taught what is necessary to apply to become free from our current way of functioning—one that, as we saw earlier, generates dissatisfaction and suffering sooner or later.

Why Take Care?

To accompany another person in an appropriate state of mind, we develop an attitude of kindness in order to access the means to be truly in relation with others. We must do this progressively, beginning from where we are and in our daily environment. It is a matter of training—training ourselves to develop discernment and kindness. Training ourselves to notice, over and over, the emotions that we experience and identify with so that we may no longer be slaves to them.

As we have seen, our emotions and mental habits condition our relationship to the world. The idea is thus to free ourselves from these obstacles. Learning to take care is an excellent way to do so. Based on correct understanding of this vision, on careful observation, and on our efforts to clarify our functioning, motivation, and resources, we move toward greater kindness.

In this way, we acquire the means to accomplish the benefit of beings while also cultivating our own benefit by keeping others' benefit in mind. It is an ambitious project, but if we limit our motivation from the start of our path, we run the risk of only seeing what we expect of the path. There is so much more to discover; we are full of intrinsic qualities that we simply need to uncover. We have the potential to achieve the complete fulfillment of these qualities; we are each endowed with this capacity. The path will be shorter or longer according to our means, but the potential is there: present, but veiled.

We all want to be happy. Each of us shares this same wish. As it seems natural for us to be happy, we can thus comprehend that it is fair for everyone to be happy. Based on this simple yet profound realization, we are then able to develop attentiveness to others and kindness toward ourselves and others.

Looking Within

To open to others—to be able to listen to them and accompany them—it is necessary to first look within at our own way of functioning. Developing awareness of what we experience—of the emotions we go through and the filters of our projections and biases—is the first step toward considering another's experience.

It may seem contradictory to begin by looking at our own way of functioning before considering others' suffering.

It is true that in a situation where we are accompanying someone, the first question we think to ask is often, "What can I do to help?" Of course, this is a good question, but often it originates in our discomfort in the face of suffering and does not take into account the effect this discomfort may have on our attitude or ability to be present with the other person. Here, we are talking about a reflection that occurs over time and not in the event of an emergency. It involves questioning ourselves with the goal of helping others.

Furthermore, taking care of ourselves also means working with our attachment to different things and ideas. We can easily observe that it is often harder to be fair minded toward our family than toward strangers. The patience we might have for someone in a professional situation evaporates when dealing with those close to us!

Madeleine, a nursing assistant in a palliative care unit, has a patient suffering from a fatal illness. Her patient is a young woman who, in her anxiety and discomfort, expresses her impatience by repeatedly verbally attacking her caregiver. Nevertheless, Madeleine continues to listen— free from anger, focused on the suffering of the young girl, and intent on soothing her. At the end of her day, Madeleine returns home to her children: two teenagers who are tired and moody after a bad day at school. It only takes fifteen minutes for Madeleine to lose patience with their repeated demands for attention!

So what's the problem? Doubtless, fatigue plays a role in Madeleine's angry reaction toward her kids. But the key point is that her attachment to her children leads to expectations, specifically behavior she feels is appropriate based on the values she is trying to teach them. This expectation hinders her from hearing their difficulties; she only hears their neediness, which disappoints her, thus leading her to respond with anger.

Based on this situation, we can understand how much our attachment to things and ideas creates limits and suffering. Hence the importance of working with our attachments in order to take care of ourselves.

This is not an easy thing, but it is through everyday situations that we can become aware of the ills of attachment. We are talking about attachment here, and not love, which obviously nurtures our relationships, especially with those close to us. Working with our attachment means recognizing and developing space around our expectations little by little. It means becoming aware of the compound and impermanent nature of all things. It means learning to love others for who they are. It does not mean forgetting about ourselves in our relationships, but instead training ourselves not to fall into the trap of the limits that attachment generates. We do this based on the wish to cultivate our own wellbeing and that of others in our relationships.

In this way, taking care of ourselves is in fact taking care of others. And being attentive to others is, likewise, taking care of ourselves. This understanding leads us to rely on our strengths, to work on our weaknesses, and to develop the resources that we lack.

Resources to Develop

Developing Clarity and Kindness

Clarity and kindness are the expression of being present. To bring them about, we need to bring together and cultivate resources that allow us to experience them in daily life. This involves developing a support mentality and a state of mind that considers others with more complexity than simply fascination and rejection or the perception of enemies and friends.

There is nothing we can do other than training ourselves in a vision that goes beyond appearances to awareness of others' experiences. Of course this vision is subjective; it is our vision of what others experience. But it is the only reality we have access to for the moment.

Accepting our situation and that of others is a precious resource. It is what allows our experiences to become a tool for transformation. We can only transform what we can accept.

This acceptance is not related to giving in to whatever happens. On the contrary, acceptance is an openness that, by nature, is the first step in a process of evolution.

By considering our difficulty with clarifying and accepting what occurs within us, we develop a kinder vision of beings who, inherently, deal with this same way of functioning. But because we can look at our own dysfunction, emotions, judgments, etc. with kindness and sympathy, we can then consider others with this same benevolence. Without kindness toward ourselves, it is difficult to be truly kind to others!

The Three Reflections

On this basis, the Buddha proposes a group of reflections that help us open to reality and make "taking care" simple. Based on progressive questioning related to our confused relationship to pleasure and dissatisfaction and interdependence and impermanence, a new discernment arises to nurture our vision.

Clarifying Our Relationship to Pleasure and Dissatisfaction

This first concerns clarifying our confused relationship to happiness and suffering. Generally speaking, we confuse pleasure with happiness and dissatisfaction with suffering. We are often prisoner to our sensations, as much physical as mental. While they inform us about situations, they simultaneously hijack our perception, though this is less the sensations themselves than the way that we relate to them. Reconsidering our relationship to how we experience things leads us to question the relevance of what we perceive.

Impermanence

A second reflection focuses on impermanence. We often relate this notion to death. If we wish to accompany people facing death or dealing with grief, of course it is important to question our relationship to suffering and death and to become aware of our mortality. But the reflection on impermanence goes further than this one angle.

To fully accomplish this reflection on impermanence, we can start with the visible effects of impermanence— observable changes. For example, the changing seasons, the blossoming of a flower, the growth of a child, the improvement or deterioration of a situation, the modernization of a country, etc.

We can become aware that, though we think of ourselves as a lasting entity at the heart of our experiences, we are actually dynamic beings in an unpredictable, continuously changing world.

Our state of mind changes, our bodies transform, and everything around us is likewise in perpetual movement.

Furthermore, reflecting on impermanence—this ceaselessly unfolding process—and contemplating the fact that things change from moment to moment allows us to better understand the way the world works. This reflection gives us access to things that our senses do not allow us to perceive.

Reflecting on impermanence leads to understanding and accepting the unpredictable nature of the situations we encounter, which decreases our fear of change. In this way, approaching others and ourselves based on the reality of impermanence enriches our understanding of situations.

All Phenomena Are Composite

All phenomena are composite. This is the third reflection. We tend to perceive objects, situations, and other people as separate and autonomous entities. In reality, everything is composite and therefore interdependent: mind and matter, emotions and the body, myself and others...

Because what is composite is interdependent, interactions have consequences. Becoming aware of interdependence and its functioning leads us to the responsibility for our actions. Once again, this allows us to be more present to reality and to relate to it with greater precision.

Consider an example. One day, you wake up late, and your morning ritual gets disrupted. Perhaps this is merely a detail, but it turns out that traffic at this late hour is heavier and on this particular day you have an important meeting! You finally get to work a half hour late and the dossier you carefully prepared the previous day is no longer on your desk... You go to see your partner on the project and discover he has the dossier. All of the frustration and irritation accumulated since your late wake-up boils over at once!

Before he can even explain himself, all of your anger spills out at him instantly...

This is a banal, ordinary situation, but it allows us to see all of the different elements that come together to create an emotional explosion. In the midst of the situation, we only register the absence of the dossier and its reappearance in the hands of someone else. We have not remotely considered all aspects of the situation. Considering the different parameters of a situation, whatever they may be, gives us a wider perspective and thus allows us to be more in touch with the situation as it is.

Furthermore, when we are angry, we experience anger

like a whole, something solid that takes us over. But if we look at our anger closely, it is a combination of sensations, emotions, concepts and of course our own conceptualization of the situation. In this way, we can once more observe the composite and interdependent nature of all phenomena.

Cultivating the Dual Benefit

Concrete tools complement the resources that we cultivate through reflection. Together, these two means lead to practicing the dual benefit: our own and that of others. This is what being present leads to. Our way of thinking, of communicating, and of acting—based on appropriate motivation and supported by attention and awareness—result in taking care of ourselves and others.

Changing Our Relationship to Disturbing Emotions

Training in being present reveals all kinds of states of mind. Some are in accord with taking care and others lead us away from it. The latter are known as disturbing emotions.

The term "emotion" itself can lead to confusion as it

does not refer to the same reality in Western psychology and in the Buddhist approach.

In this case, we are dealing with a problem of translation. In Tibetan, the word in question is *nyonmongpa*,[6] a term often translated as "disturbing emotion". It designates the states of mind that confuse the mind and create suffering.

How does this happen? First, there are the situations we encounter, and then there are our reactions to these situations. Circumstances influence our minds, which are limited by our conceptions. Due to this, disturbing emotions color our reactions. We are constantly under their influence, which sometimes leads to us encountering pleasant situations and often leads to encountering unpleasant ones.

In and of themselves, disturbing emotions are not negative if we perceive them from the moment they arise. If we do not, they lead us away from our goal. Furthermore, so long as we are under their influence, we experience constant dissatisfaction.

How do disturbing emotions arise? In the beginning, they are not more than a barely perceptible occurrence in the mind—a refusal or an attraction connected to a given

---

6   Lama Jigme Rinpoche: "There are different types of obscurations. One of them is what we call *nyonmongpa* and designates a fundamental reaction that arises in the mind based on circumstances and leads to a specific way of perceiving. This reaction elicits a way of seeing."
    See Footnote 1 for full citation and further reading.

situation. If the occurrence goes unperceived, it increases and becomes a central focus that makes us react with aversion or desire. This first occurrence—what we could call the seed of the emotion—is not harmful by nature. If we see it, invalidate it, and let it go, it becomes a source of benefit as it allows us to clarify our minds. Over the course of training, discovering this emotional seed over and over again allows us to no longer fall victim to our disturbing emotions.

The idea is not to fight against these emotions, but rather to make them part of the path. The states of mind that arise from aversion or attachment function like obscurations to the mind's natural clarity. The goal is to face them in order to use these states of mind as a tool for transformation. Working with our emotions is an integral part of taking care.

To not be subject to these disturbing emotional occurrences, we must first see them, then identify them, accept them, and not follow them. Early on in this training, we often see our emotions after the situation, sometimes a few moments after, but sometimes it takes us several days to see more clearly. This is an important step, as we can only change what we can see and accept. The view we attain of our way of functioning is in itself therapeutic; seeing our emotions with knowledge of their consequences and the suffering they bring about naturally leads us to develop the wish not to follow them. It is through patient training in this vision—and especially due to meditation—that our discernment develops and our freedom in the face of disturbing emotions increases.

Meditation

Questioning our motivation, bringing together and nurturing resources, and working with our emotions entails a means of finding inner space: meditation. Meditation allows us to develop clarity and discernment. It is a connection with ourselves—a non-mental way of knowing ourselves that also has implications for our actions. Pacifying mental agitation and experiencing greater inner stability allow us to reveal our inherent qualities. In this context, meditation accompanies every part of the process of revealing and developing the capacity to be present.

We will consider here the essential points and state of mind for meditation, but I invite you to read other works or, better yet, to receive practice instructions directly from a qualified teacher if you wish to practice meditation regularly and in a non-superficial way.

Buddhist meditation is an exercise, a method to apply in order to attain an intended goal: to liberate ourselves from suffering, to free ourselves from a limited way of functioning, and to allow each of us to realize the potential present within us. Based on an understanding of the meaning of the teaching, the practitioner learns to meditate, then trains to develop his capacity to remain focused on one point. These are the first steps of meditation training.

On the Buddhist path, meditation is not simply calming oneself, nor looking for experiences. Meditation permits the mind to not be distracted by mental habits, emotions, or conceptions that automatically arise in the mind. By developing awareness of the mind's happenings without following them—nor blocking or rejecting them—a state free from distraction allows the mind's natural clarity to reveal itself little by little.

Lama Jigme Rinpoche says, "The profound meaning of meditation is non-distraction of the mind, which is indivisible from truly being present. The mind does not get carried away, does not follow all of the occurrences (images, concepts, ideas, memories, etc.) that constantly arise within it. At the same time, mind is perfectly aware—present to itself and the world, and does not lose track of this awareness."[7]

Coming back to the meaning of putting meditation into practice, Jigme Rinpoche further clarifies, "Meditation allows us to perceive phenomena in a clear and precise way in order to be able to differentiate what is correct from what is not.

---

7 Lama Jigme Rinpoche; see Footnote 1 for full citation and further reading.

The practice of meditation leads the mind to perception without distraction: meditation dissipates inattention and—from the moment mind is less distracted—greater clarity arises. The mind is then naturally more clear."[8]

8   Lama Jigme Rinpoche; see Footnote 1 for full citation and further reading.

Conclusion

Just as we can only consider meditation in terms of training, developing the ability to be present and to take care requires training. A change in our vision of the way we function—seeing what this way of functioning entails and putting in place the means to transform it—can only occur little by little, step by step.

There is no forcing. It is a matter of looking at our mistaken attitudes gently and with kindness, conscious of the judgments that arise. We see them but do not follow them and take heart in having seen them. Because we see our errors, we can transform them, and this is heartening! "A defect we do not see is a defect, but a defect we see is a potential quality."⁹

Why work on being present and taking care? The proposition is to connect situations in which we are accompanying someone with a spiritual path by clarifying our motivation in order to give our existence a positive direction for ourselves and others. The Buddha spoke of accomplishing dual benefit: our own and that of others.

Three trainings support us and allow us to fulfill our path: ethics, meditation, and discernment.

Ethics allows us to understand how situations function and to act appropriately. This means making an effort not to cause harm and to apply what is beneficial. Taking care of ourselves means bringing together the positive conditions that allow us to help others.

Meditation is a process of connecting with ourselves based on awareness and attention. As we have seen, it allows us to pacify the mind and realize its qualities.

Discernment consists in seeing things as they are. By understanding the limits of our egocentric way of functioning—one focused solely on our own well-being, we put in place the means to become free from this way of functioning. We progressively move from partial knowledge

---

9   Gendun Rinpoche (1918–1997): A meditation master, he spent more than thirty years in retreat. The 16ᵗʰ Karmapa sent him to the West to develop Dhagpo Kagyu Ling and to create and direct lay and monastic retreat centers and hermitages to make the Dharma accessible to all. Translator's Note: This quotation comes from the author's personal archives.

to vaster knowledge that allows us to develop love and compassion toward everyone.

Based on correct ethics, taking care helps us clarify the impermanent and composite aspect of all things. Understanding the unstable nature of phenomena opens our eyes to our own capacity to transform obstacles. It allows us to harness the results of continuous transformations and to eventually establish a healthier relationship with our own mortality and that of others.

Acknowledgements

I would like to express all my gratitude and thankfulness to the lamas who have guided and guide me on the Buddhist Path: Lama Gendun Rinpoche, Lama Jigme Rinpoche, and all the masters who clarify and allow me to apply the Buddha's teaching with their teachings and advice.

I most especially would like to thank Lama Puntso, without whom this text would never have seen the light of day.

I likewise thank all the people who have helped to limit errors with their encouragement and advice.

And thank you to all those throughout my journey who have shared their knowledge and experiences. Thank you to all those who have trusted me and allowed me to walk a bit of the path by their side.

Printed in May 2017
by Pulsio

Edition Number: 0026
Legal Deposit: May 2017
Printed in Bulgaria